"ASPIRATION"

A JOURNEY OF THE SOUL

ADARSH DWIVEDI "KRISHNA"
PRIYANSHI GUPTA

Made with ♥ on the Notion Press Platform
www.notionpress.com

This book, "Aspiration - A Journey of the Soul",

is dedicated to the mother who gave me life, language and the thoughts.

Contents

Contents

Contents

Preface

Life is a journey—a winding road filled with dreams, challenges, and moments of quiet reflection. Aspiration: A Journey to Life is born from the desire to capture the essence of this journey, to celebrate the triumphs, embrace the struggles, and find meaning in the everyday.

This book is a collection of thoughts and emotions shaped by my own experiences and the stories of those who have inspired me. It is an ode to the power of hope and resilience, a reminder that every step we take is a testament to our strength and aspirations.

Through these pages, I invite you to walk with me—to explore the beauty of self-discovery, the courage of pursuing dreams, and the grace of embracing life in all its colors.

Whether you are seeking motivation, solace, or simply a moment of connection, I hope this book resonates with your heart and soul. It is my humble offering to anyone striving to live authentically and meaningfully.

Thank you for embarking on this journey with me. May it inspire you to keep aspiring, keep dreaming, and keep growing.

With gratitude,
Adarsh Dwivedi Krishna
Priyanshi Gupta.

Acknowledgements

With heartfelt gratitude, I extend my thanks to all who have walked beside me on the path that led to Aspiration: A Journey of the Soul.

To my family especially my sister, your unconditional love and faith in me have been the foundation of my strength. Thank you for being my anchor and my light.

To my friends, who lent their ears and hearts to my words, your encouragement has been the wind beneath my wings.

To the countless inspirations—life's triumphs, trials, and quiet moments of reflection—this book was born from your essence.

To my readers, your connection to these pages gives meaning to every word. May this book touch your soul as deeply as writing it touched mine.

Lastly, to the infinite universe within, thank you for guiding me through this journey of discovery and aspiration.

This book is a piece of my soul, and I am honored to share it with you.

Prologue

Aspiration is a journey of the soul—a collection of poems that traverses the landscapes of hope, introspection, love, and resilience. These verses are inspired by the raw experiences of life, capturing moments of quiet reflection and fervent emotion.

This book seeks to inspire, to console, and to challenge the reader to dream beyond the ordinary, to find meaning in chaos, and to embrace the power of aspirations. Whether it's the ache of longing, the warmth of gratitude, or the complexity of human relationships, every poem is a step closer to understanding the beauty and contradictions of existence.

Through these pages, you will encounter the world as seen through the poet's eyes: honest, tender, and unafraid to question. Let Aspiration guide you to reconnect with your dreams and the limitless possibilities within.

Welcome to the beginning of a poetic odyssey.

1. Humble goddess

Do you remember, that day,
When I came out,
I was crying,
But, you were smiling,

When I was in endless darkness,
I felt tired, with all weakness,

I called you,
I talked you,
I felt you,

I cried with your eye's,
I spoke with your voice,
You ate which I need,
For me everything you did,

When I came out, you beared pain endless,
Your smile was my celebration ,
with the freedom from darkness !
Oh!
How humble you are !

2. Smart boy

What was that day,
When I born,

No one knows, how pain,
Beared my mother, before my birth,
Might that day, my mother have fast,
When I open my eyes, in this world,
I whispered,

My mother groaning in pain, smiled,
Maid told her,
boy is born ,
So, she saw my face,
And speak with happiness,
No, Smart boy is born

3. I'll comeback

One day when I met you,
The sun was rising,
My face was shining,
One day when you walked with me
I was totally changed,
The time is silence
but there is much violence,
Actually I don't believe on you, but I believe you,
I don't want you, but I want,
you can leave me, but I can't,
When you leave I had to something say,
I tried but there was not any way,
I don't hope on you but I hope you,
you will not say me but I listen you,
Time haven't given mate after check,
believe me I'll comeback...

4. How weird

How weird
expectation and it's reality,
your word and it's morality!

thought and it's action,
faith and it's reaction !

how simple is to say, I faith on you,
but how difficult to faith in you !

actually there is the war of mind and heart,
but you think this is your smartest chart !

fair unfair doesn't matter here,
born from Mother you can ignore her tear !

how difficult to be human,
where money has much value then morality,
how can faith on you
when you take non veg and talking about humanity !

how weird, to say you man,
when you can't respect any women !

Oh lord !

How difficult this all !!

5. Human Hypocrisy

We claim,
we are human, and have humanity,
also claim,
to be sensible, but don't have sensitivity !

animal doesn't kill their baby,
before borning,
but we do and don't give chance,
to see them morning !

animal doesn't have their sensitivity,
and we claim we have humanity !

We love to known as animal lover,
we kill them, use their skin for cover !

we have much mind but more greed,
we love nature, this is only for read !

we leave our parents at old age home,
at Mother's Day have status, love you mom !

love money with have selfishness in majority,
at last we claim, have our morality !

Oh! God

How hypocrisy we have !!

6. Sometimes...

Sometimes I think to write something,
Learning the fact I think nothing.
My mind says, Are you in a comfort zone,
I say I am left with my phone .
Sometimes I think to remember something,
Learning the fact I know anything.
My mind says, Are you ready to hold,
I say I am ready to fold.
Sometimes I think to recreate something,
Learning the fact it's tough nothing.
My mind says, Are you creative?
I say I still create festive.
Sometimes I think to love something,
Learning the fact it's hurt dumb thing.
My mind says, Are you ready to suffer,
I say I am still duffer.
Sometimes I think to loose something,
Learning the fact it's a worth thing.
My mind says, Don't leave this shit,
I say it has to be made hit .

7. Opposites Attract

He was simple, she was complex.

He was quiet, she was loud.

He was Intelligent, she was non rational.

He was sterile, she was captivating.

He was smart, she was cute.

He was courageous, she was timid.

He was egoist, she was humble.

He was average, she was bright.

He was singer, she was speaker.

He was tragic, she was comic.

He was her's , she was his'.

Opposite attracts each other.

8. Journey to life....

Travelling all the way to heart
Seems there to carry the dart
Here's to another year of fare
Desiring to indulge in with care.
So many expectations, so much terror
Feeling the urge to transfer the error
Hm Bothered more to get pursuit
Mother motivated to follow the route!

9. I choose peace....

Besides party and clubs I choose nature,
To be honest I like to be mature.
Besides having everyone, i choose myself,
Having lots of laughs by herself.
Besides being extravagant, I choose simplicity ,
Sharing all the mischiefs with plasticity.
Besides being on airs, I choose vacuum,
Behaving like as all the flowers bloom.
Besides having crowd, I choose one or two.
Just like creating a wave of loo.
Besides having you, I choose me,
To the world that holds key.
Besides having discord, i choose peace,
Battling with masses to maintain pleece.

10. Someone

Someone said me, You are so dumb,
Appreciating them with a big thumb.
Someone said me, you are dark skinny,
Replying with a wide grinning .
Someone said me, You have so much scars,
Countering them by shining like a star.
Someone said me you are talentless,
Created a channel to present relentless.
Someone said me, You are the worst,
Cursed myself to be the first .
Someone said me you are futile,
Working everyday like a sutile.

11. Pleasure and Proud

In this formidable dense forest,
someone is sitting on a stone,
Some memories are in mind,
But he is fully aware,

Who's watching,
Who is celebrating the pleasure,
Leave all happiness in his home,
What, he makes new relation ,

When sky show him,
Asked his questions,
Don't you love home,
Or come here by leaving everything,

Be ready sky, you also,
I am that son of my motherland,
I love my mother,
She is everything for me,
After listening the words of soldier,
Sky also have pleasure,
Saying that too, named again,
The forest, the trees and the earth have pleasure,
And the mother have proud , proud and proud of him !!

12. You and Me

That was the day,
when I saw you,
I didn't know what happened,
but suddenly I decided
have to go long with you,

but it was not easy as much I think,
I dream you like pen and I am your ink,

This is very difficult for me to say,
you will be happy or much angry right or May,

I just passed many years without saying it to you,
but I feel unconscious when I listen which works new,

I realized that was my Blender mistake,
not that not yet but I have you to take,

your heart have broken many times that was not real,
because your real heart I have,
this is the heart please keep it safe !!

13. Dream You

Hey ,

everything is not for saying,
sometime you need to feel it,
absolutely you have doubt thoughts ,
there is no place please kill it !

when I saw the dream
you were with me,
I thought you saw same dream,
please don't judge me !

love is the beautiful thing,
it's not a war,
feel me and come fast,
don't make it far !

our past will not determine our future,
our present will determine it,
the task is to live life with future,
don't leave, be with me and assign it !!

14. Gratitude

When I opened my eyes, in this new world,

I was unknown, I could have been die,
If my mom not bring me, I only cry !

Mom gave me knowledge of language,

She was my first teacher,
it was my pleasure,
You all give me knowledge of subject and life,
This is also my pleasure !

I thanks my all known teacher's
which are in my mind,
I also thanks all unknown teacher
who are behind the mind !

I don't have much word, to gratitude you,
With good feelings I say,
Thank you !!

15. Truth

When, I born ,
You decided me to live ,
It's true ,
you will take, back which you gave,

The whole purpose of life is.
to archive divine soul,
Have that much time,
Till I am in role ,

It is the journey between,
divine energy to divine energy reservoir
Between this all materialistic things are liar,

Karma's of morality will help you,
To achieve your goal,
Remember this is like drama ,
You have to play your role,

At last you will have to marry with the goddess of death,
This is realty other things are only myth.

16. And the day comes..

Awaited hundred days for the result,
Felled a guilt of insult.
A feeling of discontentment in nerves
Thinking that will I someday deserves
Mother flouting the worst
Waiting for the day to burst
Excitement broked down in a minute
Reasoning when will I then remet
A boy and a girl dreamed of a suit
Everything seems cute and was ever mute.

17. Am I unlucky?

Everyday hearing he/she cleared this,
Myself wondering why always her/ his .
Always worked hard the same
Why I was not the main.
Everyday hearing she was awarded this
Sensing I was also in the wishlist .
Always saw a failure with no. 1 or 2 .
Will this continue forever too .
Everyday hearing he/she was praised.
Amazed at myself I also raced .
Everytime unlucky the priyanshi,
Will she be ever the gods anshi.

18. Life is no one's friend

Who says tomorrow is happier
I had seen people getting scrappier
Who says tomorrow' is luxury
I had seen people getting blurry
Who says tomorrow is rich
I had seen people being ditch
Who says tomorrow will be better
I had seen people getting closer to deader
Who says tomorrow you can be famed
I had seen people who have been gamed.
Who says tomorrow will be the best
I had seen people resting with the pest
"Live for today because tomorrow is not a light for everyone."

19. Acne : A part of life

Acne became an organ of her life
Always thought to become it's knife
Becoming knife became a threat
Accepted it as a summer's wet.
Acne hated normals, but adored the filters ,
Said bye to camera and welcomed snap litters
She said snaps you are okay,
But the snaps also shows the way.
Hating everyday became a suicide
But loving everyday became a pride
Ceased to treat as a knife ,
She smiled and said it was her life.

20. "If You Think You Cannot, Think Again"

If you think you cannot be a writer,
just give only half an hour to become a fighter.
If you think you cannot be a dancer ,
just learn two steps to become like a freelancer.
If you think you cannot be a singer,
just play the Spotify feels like a zinger(outstanding person)
If you think you cannot be a painter
just stain the wall and feel like you are a skyscraper
If you think you cannot be a vocalist,
just argue once and feels like a journalist.
If you think you cannot be a politician,
just oppose everything and feel like as you are a tactician .
If you think you cannot be a comedian,
just dress up like a mad and feels like a demon

21. Friends

First radiation in earth never dies,
Friends are mine or they are lies.
Someone told me, they are the best
And someone told they are the test.
Correlating me with them was a messing,
But associating me with one was a blessing.
Friends really exist in my gallery .
But finding among them was 'you'a Valery.
Who says friends are worthless or poison
I find them as a chicken with lemon
Wishing everyone a happy friendship day.
But longing for 'you' will be a pray.

22. To Young man

Hey, young man today I met your father,
He was sick, alone, weak and other,
It's look good that you settled down,
Without son, a father got moral down,
Your mother was also suffering from bad of health,
But who cares you managed your Wealth.

Might you have forgot your parents face,
But who cares, you have enough cash.
My friend don't come if you buy
Son for your mother,
Don't come if you buy some time
For your father,
Come, if you want to see smile on their face,
It's time to be with parents not in money race.

Oh, My friend
Remember moral values!

23. Memories

Ever when I be with silence
Take deep breath
For countering internal violence
Some memories heat me
Like stone
Some upsets me like I lost
They won.

When I remember crowd
Realise how alone,
Nobody understand this pain
For me it's known
I am so angry but looking calm
Body has cold, blood is warm
I faith you but you are tied
For you everything is wide,

Ups and downs are the part
It's come and go,
But memory heat me like aim
And they are arrow
I don't know you faith me or not
But I have something it's what

Silence and narration
Thoughts Without expression

24. To my friend

After a long time I found,
I look slowly and moved around
My desire to her changed for her
Love came in light lust gone blur,

I decided to walk with you,
It was my dream not anything new,
You love to see moon I love to see
I am like river on noon and you as sea.

Your eyes are so deep and silence
It's look calm but have much violence
We have faith and freedom to say
Someone controlled you by killing that ray

Our connection is with unconscious mind,
Without presence I see, it's not blind,
I live inside your dreams and heart,
Can't kicked me out even you do new start,

When you went you looked your future,
Not angry it's times nature!!

Oh my friend

Be happy!!

25. Our Hypocrisy

One word humanity,
Is for humans
Although we claim to have
But we don't…
We claim to love animals
But mutton we want,

Goat never try to eat our baby
But we do
Then says to others
What do, not to do…

We have conduct of animal rights
But love to eat chicken,
We lost our moral
This is our greed began,

We want only money and satisfy our lust
Forget our duty and selfishness have must
Kill own baby and have morality lost,
Then we also claim
we want to save the nature at any cost!

Oh God

How hypocrites we are!

26. To you

<u>To you</u>

Do you remember that day
When you met me
When you asked me
What do you want
I felt nervous just thought
I can't
Your eyes were deep but questions like arrow
Had much to say but did small and narrow

For first time when we walked together
We felt some connection
To enjoy the weather.

Do you remember that day
When you realised
that have faith and love
It's about moments and relation
Not only rub

Love doesn't allow to be selfish
It makes me kind
It's free nature
Not bind

But, when you gone
I just watched and cry
Do you think I still have
That feels
It's not lie !!

27. Apathy

Haven't you think of a person who is yours
Seems to have a world that has no cures
Had to suffer all the way solitary
Always had a vision to be like a tree.
Trust was a miracle, but became pointless
Did this happens to everyone or only left me homeless.
Sharing efforts all became a venom
Will this was a return of demon.
Never imagined a world like it
Will this continue forever like pits
Dreams transformed from trust to crust
Will I be rosted into it like the rust.

28. Is it okay to hurt ??

The world has paced to the next generation ,
Really will she continue with the hibernation
Never mind, sometimes she does the good job
And sometimes she ignores the big mob.
Hurting was never her intention,
Maintaining the decorum was her prevention,
Never mind sometimes she has a skepticism
And sometimes she has a trust Aestheticism
Her heart speaks all 50/50 words
Ignoring the fact will it hurt like gird
Eager to know her illness for her cut
Then God says it is okay to hurt!

29. Random thoughts

Thinking of you was a routine,
And everything seems so serene
Time passed as smooth as silk
Searching you nowhere was a guilt
Willing to feel the shell of yours
Desire to get the dull of cures
Chattering an hour to cure the lust
Felled a sense of solace and have the bust.

30. Isn't she strange?

A girl with no limits always doubts
Haven't you think why she shouts
Let's play a magic game to guess
Game didnt work , you came to know less
She cares for her comfort, she left all her shirts
She cares for her pride, she without reason hurts .
Let's play sudoku to understand her
Numbers disappeared as a bird's fur.
She loves to win, but she hates to lose
She loves to aid but she hates to be restrained
Let's play a black and white game to umpire
She Unknowingly plays to become a liar.

31. The day after new eve

Once again with a fresh year
Having dreams just like a day dear,
Have to make it a golden one
Who says it's not done!
Let's try one more time
And hit it like a bell chime!
No more trying making it
Only doing to achieve it ,
This year is a chance
Yes I'll make it my dance

32. Whispers of solitude

Sitting under the shadow of tree
Not having friends makes me always free
My soul asked is it okay?
The leaves whispered and said it is your way
Trusting the way was a reality check
Hanging with the people was only a beg
My soul asked will you continue
The flowers said it fools like glue

33. Lest we forget

Counting him in the stars
Days are passing and the feelings still alive
The sorrows are in the heart
But memories overflow when the generations dive
Years gonna pass with age
Defending that magical love with the last breath
Still counting a family full of cage
Doesn't this the real indicator of death.
Missing you every year is an era
Legends never die was the caption
Ain't we count you always as a chutepara
Baba, you were always a legend in our actions.

34. Confused why i met you?

Wandering all along the streets,
Met everyone who gave me treats
Suddenly crashing with you
And God gave me a cue.
Wasn't that an unimaginable meet
Creating choas in the minds if I cheat
Ohh heaven grace shed light on me
If I open the doors with a locked key

35. Evil eye ascendant

Who knows she was bright
But her mouth uttered it right
Highlighted the capacity of her
Didn't realised the falling prey of evil eye.

36. A dream

Don't you know who?
I remain silent in my thoughts
What should I say to you?
It looks like I don't like you
This relationship is so deep
How to understand that she is an angel
Hearts love each other again and again
That's a long way, man!
Still it feels like you
Talks has also happened to us
My memories are filled with memories of dreams.
Is it my fault or yours, I don't understand

37. Her chosen peace

Always distressed
But why?
Haven't she have to handle all the class chores,
Or she intentionally get bores.
Haven't she receives all the headaches ,
Or she knowingly makes mistakes.
Everyday she counters with one or the other,
The rhythm she heals to be with her mother.
A decision was taken
With full shaken
"Let's enjoy always to be alone
Matching your vibe with your own. "

38. Isolation

A girl with the set boundaries
Had to suffer all the way like laundry
She is all helpless
How to handle her mess
Economically hardship
Way of living being cheap
Unsounding everyday
Wanted to fly faraway?
Dreaming high
Without resource being sigh
Felt guilt inside
Bound with limitations cried,,..

39. A part of life

Loosing everyone each day makes me more close to god
Looking the sky and wondering it the world to shook
Everyone has a reason to smiles
And myself has only option to reach to miles
Let's take a chance to grab the moment
And I know I will work with the silent.
Worries apart, good going ahead .
I know success will be spread.

40. Did you made attempts??

Did you made attempts??
I try to meditate but lot of confusions was in mind
I try to convince but the cure went in reverse
I try to speak but the words get moulded to vague
I try to think but the thoughts perenigrate itself
I try to clarify but everything was obscure.
I try to notice around but i find everything to be double faced.
I tried to made attempts but i failed.

41. Anybody

Is anybody here
Who have heart
for loving each other

Anybody here ?
Who have courage
To be human

Anybody Here?
Who have guts
To help others

Anybody here?
Who want to listen
story of those
Who could not speak.

Anybody here?
Who thinks for others
Those who don't have resources.

Anybody here?
Who want to support
Those who lost their hope.

Is anybody here?
Who can be free
Those who have hunger rope !

Support if you are human
For humanity
Tell if you are able
It's our responsibility!!

42. Why worried?

Time is demanding, don't wait
Lean into the noisy time
The soul is filled with conflict
The world is telling you to be afraid

set out to win everywhere
But they were already defeated in the battle
Blood on the face, blood in the heart too
You were afraid and lost your life,

But is defeat the reason for fear?
or the things of the world,
Cowardice is in the mind
or are you afraid to fight,

that once fell to the earth
gave up getting up again
Frightened by the thorns
turned his face from his path

But in living as a coward
Doesn't death come every day?
lowered eyes, lowered shoulders
Is this not the death of the mind?

If you are alive then get up now
stop worrying about delirium
Leave your fear, sleep and laziness here
sing the song of battle again

one day gold will be on the embers
So why be afraid of thorns?
death is the ultimate truth
Then why be afraid of it now?

43. To your Believe

Hey listen

I am trying to say something
can you hear me,

It is truth that I have not tell so much things,
But literally I can fly even I don't have wings.

Is there necessary to say you everything.
Without saying you won't know anything.

It is true you know the things are
Because you can read my face,
I tell you or not it doesn't matter
I am always in race,

Believe in your believes
it will help you to achieve your goal,
Everything is not written
your Karma's will also play their role,

You know I am not saying anything
You feel and listen everything ,

If you claim that you know me
If you cliam you believe me

If you have the faith on your Karma's,
If you have the work,
which have you done,
So Don't fear don't worried
You will achieve your destiny without losing one,

Oh my friend
it is very funny to say you something with silence,
Oh God how much I have violence,

44. Faith beyond boundaries

You know,

When I saw you
with culture tradition,
how attracted you me,
I can't mention !

I feel my believe is also yours,
without thinking I can't live, this is my inner force !

your beer on is not only reason to want you,
this is only the excuse,

I also faith in your nature and tradition,
this is nothing just a good news !

physically you are so far for me
but your picture is in my mind,
I like, but not as a blind !

Colour doesn't matter,
this is not new,
I faith on your nature, believe in you !

Oh!

" Krishna" feels the soul !!

Poet - Adarsh Dwivedi "Krishna "

45. Never Give up

I won't give up, I won't give up,
If memories come, come,
If things go, go
The wind will blow, the message will say,
Tell me then, I will know their condition
I won't give up, I won't give up !

By living in these memories,
Why was I so restless
I am mother's darling
Without her my mind was stunned !

the armour of his blessings,
Take your dagger of memories,
Get up, go ahead,
get a chance to meet her !

Make restlessness a weapon
Make speed his edge,
I will give full strength,
And I'll know it by distinguishing it,
I will not give up, I will not give up!!

46. Village Peace

Ever
I thought about the feel of peace,
I go in deep and imagine about my village ,
where the sun rises with the happiness,
and down with knowledge !

when I imagine this all.
my face seems like happiness call !

there is the temple in the middle of village,
that is the centre of deep self knowledge !

if you have faith on yourself, so you can feel the energy of nature ,
this is nothing,
but the power of the culture !

now in the city have much comfort,
everything can be available here !
Except, mind peace and moral values !!

47. My Hope

Hey
my hope,
please be continue with me,
why are you trying to leave me,
don't break my heart,
have some faith on me,
the dreams which have we seen together,
please don't discontinue,
don't change like weather,
you know which is the hope,
The last Faith of life,

Hey
my hope,
please be continue with me,
why are you trying to leave me,
don't break my heart,
have some faith on me,
the dreams which have we seen together,
please don't discontinue,
don't change like weather,
you know which is the hope,
The last Faith of life,

48. Dream

A dream in which she is with me,
A dream in which there is a mother's feeling,
To see a dream,
To throw stones together,
The wave that rises in the water by throwing stones,
A dream to contain them in your heart,

My dreams are your dreams or should I say our dreams,

dream of life,
dream of closure,
of dream,
dream of love,

our dreams and our dreams

49. Aim of life

In this deserted room.
a boy is sitting alone and thinking,

what happened.
if there is darkness Kingdom,
it doesn't mean,
light does not exist in this world !

if most one is greedy in this world,
doesn't mean all moral values we have lost,

one ray of light is enough for endless darkness Kingdom
for that you have to pay cost !

mortality is the last truth of nature,
your body will end, this is your future !

then why greed and selfishness ??
Acquire knowledge and defeat darkness !

energy never end it's only transform,
leave your endless greed and have values
your thoughts will never die,

they always perform !!

50. Love

Love is the thing which make your life beautiful.
this is the colour which make you colourful,
When you have this, you respect everyone,
Your love is for humanity, not only for one,

This feeling of love and lust are not same,
One makes your life for humanity,
Other for one name,

It never ties anyone, allows to free with nature,
Other tries to control everything, also tight your creature,
They take attraction, affection and lust like love,
But they tie, want only near about rub,

Love give faith and faith gives hope,
They are connected with other,
But there is no tight rope |

A Journey Shared

This collection of poetry is a labor of introspection, emotion, and reflection—a journey through the myriad landscapes of the soul. Each poem in this book is a fragment of lived experiences, observations, and dreams that have shaped my understanding of life and its profound complexities.

To those who have found pieces of their own journey within these pages, I offer my gratitude. Poetry thrives not in isolation but in the shared space between writer and reader. Your interpretations, your feelings, and your connections breathe life into these words beyond what I could imagine.

As this journey of aspiration concludes on paper, let it ignite within us the courage to embrace the journey of our souls. May these verses inspire you to reflect, to dream, and to aspire—ever onward, ever upward.

Thank you for accompanying me on this path.

With love and gratitude,

A.D. "Krishna"

www.ingramcontent.com/pod-product-compliance
Lightning Source LLC
LaVergne TN
LVHW041235150826
845673LV00008B/2387
9798896739449